COVER ART CREDIT : FREEPIK.COM

Merry Christmas
gift
FUN
happy New Year

Merry Christmas

New
Year!

2018
Happy New Year!

party
happy
2018
xmas
celebration

2018
Happy New Year!

HAPPY
2018

Merry
CHRISTMAS

Merry
Christmas

GET FREE OUR COLORING PAGES and Promotion Update

At : bit.ly/get_gift_coloring

Insects Collection Coloring Book

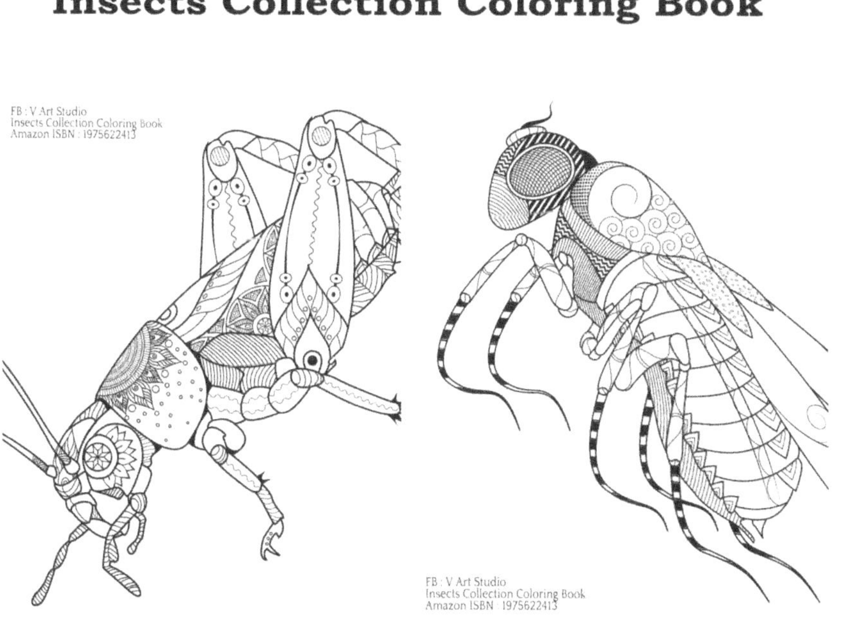

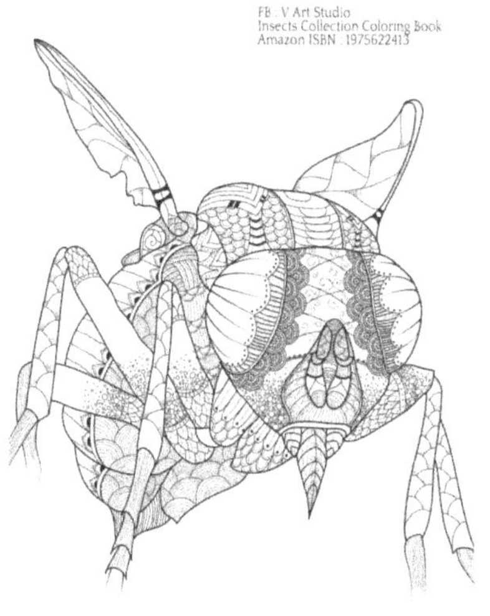

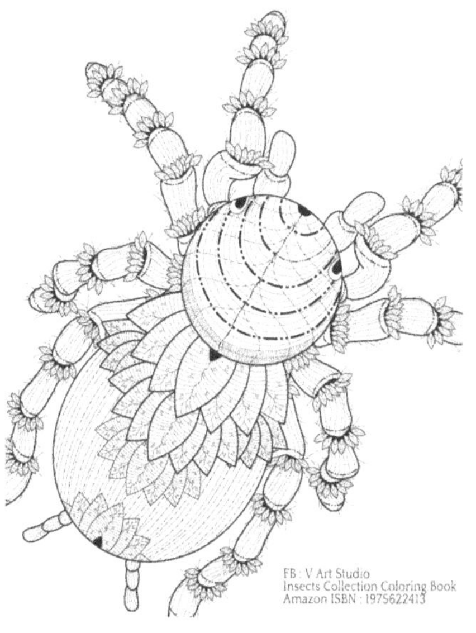